clay eyes | Tyler Blanski

All poetry by Tyler Blanski

ISBN 978-0-6151-9405-9

© 2008   Tyler Blanski
© 2008   Ezekiel Records and Creative Group
         2751 Hennepin Ave S #230
         Minneapolis, MN, 55408

All rights reserved. Unauthorized duplication is a violation of applicable laws. Permissions: tyler.blanski@gmail.com

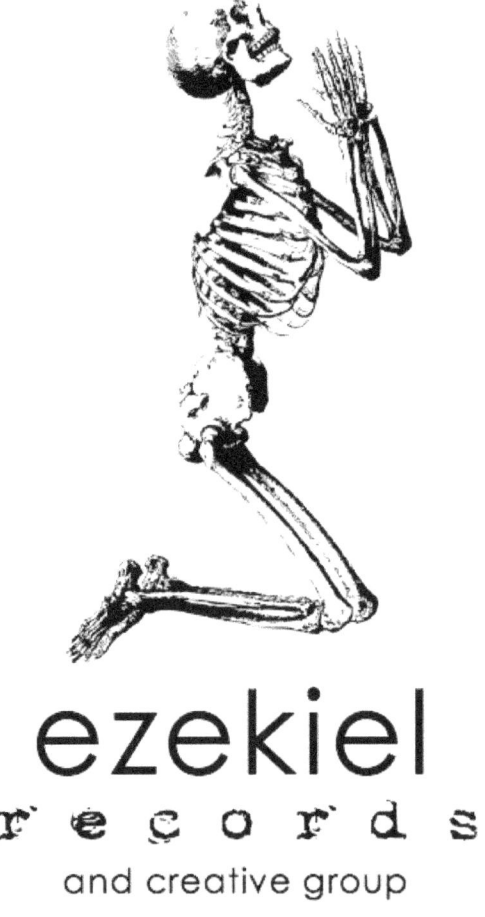

ezekiel
records
and creative group

clay eyes

clay eyes | Tyler Blanski

clay eyes | Tyler Blanski

a poetry collection by
Tyler Blanski

clay eyes | Tyler Blanski

clay eyes | Tyler Blanski

table of contents

739	13
God bent in the garden and kissed him	14
i haven't the faintest; none	15
this poem is not for lovers	16
Shoulder	17
Vox Clamentis	18
The house at Pooh corner	19
To a virgin on virginity	20
Dei plena sunt omnia	21
Sanctity	22
The Eastern Gate	23
A Dissertation	24

On the hills where cinnamon grows	26
Asking for Eggs	27
The Divine Conspiracy	28
Where the silent hymns of heaven grew	29
Very happy—grateful, even	30
Naked, and	31
36	32
Who will war?	33
Self	34
Bells to kill the dead	35
Star strewn	36
(existential question)	37
44	38
Love (hence, life)	39
16	40
House painting	41
Dearly	42
Life, select quotes	43
Lemons	44
If art would be love	45
Transplanting	46

Memento Mori	47
when every critic is a cricket	48
Uz	49
Supplicant	50
27	51
A faerie for every boy and girl	52
a guggenheim dates an artist	53
stratocaster stratosphere	54
Coupling	55
King David's Dance	56
Late the candle burns	57
Clobbering father wings	58
I wanted to tell you	59
i heard around a whispering	60
Individual, individual	61
Senior citizens	62
Cedar	63
My brother's hands	64
None righteous; no, none	65
Be thou now my only	66
Rocks to moan and clench	67

clay eyes | Tyler Blanski

We are born old; we must try to die young.

clay eyes | Tyler Blanski

clay eyes | Tyler Blanski

739

love is
do not forget to laugh!
smiles stack like road miles past,
pastels and paintbrushes and love rushes,
scars, are better than men's photographs
ten times ten their in degrees and screens.

'slur, are you In love?' they would ask,
amiInlove. plotting points wherethere is nogrid. she is.
she is no coordinates of parabola.
dinner burnt: shirts unmending: overspending:
smiles am i In love!
listen to her:
her body (already) bears the marks of time, stars, ,

throw yr five pedal flowers to the air
and punch the man who stares :
she is no picture;
she is no metered sonnet;
she is;

clay eyes | Tyler Blanski

God bent in the garden and kissed him

If you saw the flies
wander the taught yellow skin,
and if you smelled the ovens;

if you felt
the ribbons of flesh
harrowed across a slave's broad back;

and if you heard a girl
scream and bleed when soldiers
line up between her splayed legs

you would not be so quick to liken
human utterance and human art to a primate's sign language;
you would hear how hollow the old lie rings,
Ethics is an adaptation for the survival of the species.

clay eyes | Tyler Blanski

i haven't the faintest; none.

i haven't the faintest; none.
the sky, the world, the pregnant girl;
the smell of autumn and leaves ready for kicking
on roadsides and in liturgies; rural
church days (and every all days) say:
'i and these my own are for you.'
and i know you:
you're the place i've been walking towards.

all the king's men and the horses thereof
fixed in their orbits, by and by, by love.
her abdomen, her neck, the swale of her back and then…
harvest time, hardware stores, lemon trees and monasteries
say: 'i and these my own are for you.'
and i know you:
but I haven't the faintest; none.

clay eyes | Tyler Blanski

this poem is not for lovers,

though it will harm not a one of them:
young and older hearts: be boring!

a titanic insight, a morning storm
thunderbolt that strikes you when you're shaving

is the least of things love is.
i see no reason for anything less

than carefully, patiently, yes, critically
loving the vagaries unorthodoxly.

shoulder

mis-, de-, ex-,
un-poetry, all gone:
Christ does not remember:
why do you, remade and shining
ad-, re-, in-,
pro-soul?

comely believes nothing
he cannot measure or weigh.

'how much does yr wife weigh?'
i asked, 'and how does she measure?'

~~kisses~~, ~~love make~~, ~~fiery tongues~~, all gone:
in nomine Patris et Filii et Spiritus Sancti,
how much does she weigh?

Vox Clamantis
…And Nicodemus said to Him, 'How can these things be?'
   —John 3

Religion? Wait. Dance with me.
If you weren't so serious, I'd take you seriously.
Give this vintage time to breathe…
Come tomorrow: we'll put on our domesticity,
And work this out on the front porch
With a pack of cigarettes.
Then I'll whisper what I've heard,
Then I'll pour the wine:
All of Heaven is after me, I know it.
I will not die until I have broken
The bread and tasted the wine—
Until I am wet with water.

The house at Pooh corner

That they may be one, as you and I are one.
—John 17

Honey is made
from all sorts of flowers, immortaling flowers,
flowers all looking at the sun:

the bees are making honey
from all sorts of flowers, thirsty flowers,
flowers all praying for the rain:

and Pooh is in his honey jar,
thinking about all sorts of honey, licking honey,
loving honey, not thinking about flowers at all,

singing ditties to the bee.

clay eyes | Tyler Blanski

To a virgin on virginity

I could say your chaste breast wasn't made for worms to taste,
Nor your body patient shaped for a ghost's good pleasure;
And since our romping bed is too exhaustive to fit inside a coffin,
My laydee! Kiss me while our limbs still have blood in them!

But, no: first fruits, however bright, too soon plucked are never ripe,
And death reminds us we are not made for each other.
So let not our eager hearts yet beat behind bedroom doors shut tight,

And I'll kiss you everywhere in my mind as I walk you home tonight,
I'll only hold your hand and wish you the loveliest sweetest sleep tonight.

Great God! I won't be ~~nineteen~~ ~~twenty-one~~ twenty-four forever!

clay eyes | Tyler Blanski

Dei plena sunt omnia

all the world is quiet tonight
and though his stigmata still bleeds
St. Francis is asleep, and the black sheep
leaps over the moon while Brother Ass
laughs and the Mona Lisa weeps
a Martha's weep. hope expects,
trust possesses, (but Love does mess, wreck
and breathe): Martha,
Martha, do you believe?
   Who hangs upside down with St. Peter?
   lines and cross-hatches and matches
   Who holds his clothes, not wears them, with St. Francis?
   a martyr's tasteless classless
        clockless Martha's
'Yes Lord: I believe.'

clay eyes | Tyler Blanski

Sanctity

Learn to listen, not to wait.
By spittle and pity are great saints made, not
Long walks, eloquent talks, and solitary caves.

Not with gold, traditions old, or a prepossessing nave
Is purgatory and the road to heaven paved,
But with graffiti, cracked sidewalks, St. Valentine's Days.

Learn to listen and to wake
A thousand times a thousand days
To house mice—not the general agreement

On tariffs and trade—
But to pigeons and sparrows
(For the All is white and unspent).

Then you'll see men:
They might look like trees,
But they are walking—

The Eastern Gate

...Till they rest in Thee.
—St. Augustine

We sparkle, we chaff
And in tones nonchalant but grim
Confess the therapy of rosaries
Adultery and gin.
But, Oh, love, do not look me in the eye!
Morning's torso always turns, always redresses in disgrace.
Lift the fig leaf to the face
(we can't go back the Eastern way):
Conquest, rapture, boredom's salted taste,
And bead by bead, dismisséd grace
Slips
From our fingers, from our bed,
And, disenchanted, sighs upon the floor.
The unheard didactic
Was invitation to adore.

A DISSERTATION
Aurora Borealis, Aurora Australis[1]

We are, I am told, evolved[2] star powder:
The explosion, the exodus, the slow growth—
Our anatomy[3] is a little cosmology.[4]
No wonder a firmament[5] fills the cerebrum:[6]
Expanses stretch inside us, aromas,[7]
Our thinking caps are knit by Mother Reason,
Person sets a match to the soma;[8]
No wonder we wish our city lights,
The spirit of Claudius,[9] wouldn't
Curtain like a cloud[10] the night sky.

The epidermis[11] is not the terminus:[12]
The soul outside-looking-in,
Inside-looking-out,
Moves back and forth,
Forth and back again,
In and out of the viscera:[13]
We are permeable,[14] porous;
And, to some degree, the world within us
Is also the world around us
(we call this *aura*).[15]

God walks in the garden,
In the cool of the evening;
His potter Spirit throws auricles, cleaving,
And blows upon the waters, breathing;
He roves upon the dawn.

¹ a phenomenon of light in the sky, caused by charged particles from the sun interacting with atoms in the atmosphere. In northern and southern regions it's called aurora borealis and aurora australis [*borealis* is from Latin, *'northern,'* based on the Greek *Boreas*, the god of the north wind; *australis* is from Latin, *'southern,'* from *Auster 'the south, the south wind.'*]; poetic/lit. "the dawn".
² to develop from simple to more complex over successive generations, often as a result of natural selection.
³ the branch of science concerned with human body structure; the physical structure of a person.
⁴ the science of the origin and development of the universe, esp. the "big bang theory," which combines observational astronomy and particle physics; an account or theory of the origin of the universe.
⁵ the heavens or the sky, esp. when seen as a tangible thing; fig. a world viewed as a collection of people.
⁶ the principal part of the brain, located in the front of the head, made up of two hemispheres. It's responsible for the integration of sensory and neural functions and regular activity in the body.
⁷ a subtle, pervasive quality or atmosphere; a distinctive, pleasant smell.
⁸ the body as distinct from the soul and mind.
⁹ the antagonist in Shakespeare's *Hamlet*.
¹⁰ a mass of condensed water vapor floating in the atmosphere; fig. a state or cause of gloom and worry.
¹¹ the outer layer of cells covering a person.
¹² a final point in space or time; an end.
¹³ the organs in the abdomen; the intestines.
¹⁴ allowing liquids or gases to pass through it.
¹⁵ an atmosphere or quality that seems to surround a person; an emanation surrounding the human body; the essence of the individual.

On the hills where cinnamon grows
"turn my beloved and show yourself..."
        —Song of Solomon

some say
Jesus somewhere's
 not a handsome man/ a lovely man, etc.,
(such aestheticism etc. isms
   shave a hard bewhiskered/
   home-from-battle captain figure;
   dress a brave audacious naked/ /
   smooth rumpled homespun winter kissing sheets),
                                          and cough.
i say
Why iron Eve's fall-time leaves?
Why hack at appled Adam trees,
reAdamed trees, and a beautiful groom,
and a quiet room with curtains;
and a woman wearing only a pear,
asking lamp posts for rhymes for me?

and laydee
 see how street lights fight for thee?
 see how his limbs and eyes are lovely?
 see thou how his knees, his bruised knees/
 the hours and the sea/ / the lions and the roses
 and the honeybees call for thee?
   and he is handsome, and he is beautiful,
       and he is summer, and he is rain,
       and he is all the children leading/
       a vast army behind Aslan's mane.

Asking for Eggs

Our When and Who and Art in Heaven
On earth as in how forgotten Will be done?
I am sheep and child and clay,
And ought all smiles be;
With all debts paid, dancing daily bread,
This day forgiven by thy name.

Lead not but deliver us—
Wanting fish, knocking on doors,
Asking for eggs,
Learning to forgive trespasses still.
For thine is the When and Where
And How and Why forever
And wherever, Amen.

clay eyes | Tyler Blanski

The Divine Conspiracy

I'm afraid that if I surrender everything
I'll have to choose between Africa and India
Or face the fishes like a stubborn Jonah;
That if I make God's will my will
He'll go changing my perspective,
Trick me into marrying a tuba
With a beautiful heart; that one day
I'll wake with a start, next to the oompah,
In Africa or India, and be happy in my sorry state!
I like my America! I like a woman's shape!

clay eyes | Tyler Blanski

Where the silent hymns of Heaven grew

Since God does not grow old,
And truth is always new,

Let every adult stoop low, peel back
The great wonderment behind every Fact.

Pianists in all things hear sound and rhythm;
Painters from everywhere perceive color, expression;

Poets all over see simile and letters,
Like children learning to translate silence:

Who else will break the surfaces of things
To the throbbing heart of Being,

Where every body drips with dew,
Where the silent hymns of Heaven grew?

There is treasure locked there,
And all artists fumble with the keys,

Like old martyrs on their knees.
But if they could what martyrs knew,

clay eyes | Tyler Blanski

I am very happy—grateful, even

I am very happy—grateful, even—for mechanical simile
Which allows heart surgeons to perform surgery.

But if any man dares bring into my lover's bed
(sneaking into lecture halls and the back of my head),
words like *screw, function, vibrate, lever,* or *automatic,* may his head be shaved bald
and may his mouth be stuffed with threads and cotton balls!

Thank God for the feminine mystique and the lion that is Woman.
Thank Him, even, for sexual independence and freedom.

But if sex sinks to sexism, and all things feminine to feminism chic
She can keep her cashmere quilts and 600 single-ply thread count sheets,
Her tips, tactics, strategies, and secrets/ How To make love heels-over-head
—bloodless substitutes all compared to my laydee's threadbare bed.

God bless the car mechanics, the doctors, and the plumbers:
salt, hammers, and hardwood lumber/ they're something of bread and butter.

But if they stoop to mechanism, scientism, or plumbism,
may they keep locked up in their own little houses their clockwork cosmos.
My laydee is all dark valleys and the Spring/ all mountains and the sea is she,
And for this I am very—grateful, even—happy.

clay eyes | Tyler Blanski

Naked and

In the morning
When we wake
You're a warm,
Deep fever.

Your ores, impurities,
Clean water:
I try always to dig
Past the clay.

You taste
Like sun and rain.
The harvest's yield,
The field, and the unmade day

Wait on our make,
Wait for our rendering.
You wear mortality
Like a garment

But you are, like you were,
More the horror,
The hurrah, the hallowed,
More the beautiful

Naked and eternal.

36

we don't believe
the world is flat, like a giant table

but only because we fell off too late and can't get back.

w e   li ve   o n   c   r   u   mb   s .

clay eyes | Tyler Blanski

Who will war?

Must we be scattered,
Scattered like seed to sow,
To walk the Wide World thick with foes?
How trodden under foot, how forgotten,
Is the joy and strength of bodies:
They are no more or less than Christ,
Christ hid in coarse and common Christian life.

There is no such sacrament for the scattered lonely,
The sick, imprisoned, exiled, travelers sowing.
With night closing in,
And with still some great distances to go,
They have no hailing benediction
To cheer them on a cold and weary way home.
Who would not his fireside leave,
His comfortable half finished verses,
To brave the treacherous snows,
To follow without camaraderie,
And into the violent abuses go?
Who would not the letter heed that pleads,
'Timothy, in my last hour come to me'?

One's own heart is oft uncertain,
A brother's heart is sure:
We are, one another, postmen of salvation,
Lights when darkness the heart immures.
And so How good it is and how pleasant, sings
The poet, For lads to live together.
But we must be scattered,
Scattered like seed to sow.

Self

Let us go back up the whirligig toy of history
to when occult ties yet yoked the body's
humours with herbs and animals, lunar tides;

to when the stars were not so alone: before 'Cogito,
ergo sum,' and before *conscience* and *duty* were personified:
back up the merry-go-round of history let us

to when *improvement* meant still 'to till wasteland'/ was not yet spliced
with *self-* (and before every other *self-*this and *self-*that knickknack):
before 'progress' and 'evolution' and the 'great march of history,'

to when *silly* held its old meaning, 'blessed': let us,

if but for a moment, put down our diaries and look
at all the trolls, goblins, elfs, pixies, and pucks/
escape our-selfs, our self-conscious synapses and cells:

if but for a moment.

Bells to kill the dead
It is a trustworthy statement...
—2 Timothy

He had fire in his belly
And a bell to wake the dead.
It spreads out, even now, like morning,
The hammer-ringing in my stead.
It rings, it coughs—rings its frightful toll:
Though now awake, God was dead
And I am drinking water, chewing leaven bread.

Bread upon the waters,
Water off a duck's back.
Did the Jawbone Spirit work like yeast in me?
The knell (God, the knell), pounds upon my intractable quack,
Two eye sockets gazing blindly on a laughing room.
Bells, forge clay eyes; give this rough draft
Strength to make the room collapse.

clay eyes | Tyler Blanski

Star strewn

I once filled a mason jar
With shooting stars
And buried it in my backyard.

I dug for the treasure,
Years later,
Only to find a jar of letters,

Of 'I love you,'
'But if this winter proves you,'
And 'Write me How and Why.'
The inevitable 'I've wronged you.'

Why take pictures of sound?
Why try the sky to capture underground?
Are thrown stars ever found—
No matter how framed, or for whatever reason?
Why write High Art, Self Expression, and Memories down?
Memorials—Not even:
Let dead letters spread their own ashes 'round.

I can only her love now, in this only season.

clay eyes | Tyler Blanski

(existential question)

hey mr,   is there detergent enough
                and quarters and such?

my laydee, i neither know nor see
            but if you put your underwear
            on your head and if you show me how
            to fold your bras when I do the laundry
            perhaps then we'll unravel this mystery.

44

We really are on the tail end of things. We are likely the last generation. The days of history are near done. Soon we will probably roll over and die—The great corps of humanity, The great corpus of the literati, The corbel of the common happy. Would not the sun collapse With no eyes to see him, No tongue to praise him? Or would he and the whole world sigh in relief And get on with things? Would not our plumbing and our concrete Remind the lilies and the plains, The bison lolling in the brown, That we were truly great? That everyone after Shakespeare memorized Shakespeare? That we could put a harness to horses, wind and oil, the sun? Or does none of it matter? When we roll over and die So will Satan and God. The world will move on.

No, much worse: though late, We are very much new. The only is there is is now. The days of history have really just begun. We will successively roll over into eternity (Jesus doesn't throw a thing away), and the The joy of Heaven isn't obsequious, Endless entertainment and praises. How odd: We will successively roll over into eternity, The great healing bathhouse of Heaven, And there we will find baskets of gauze, Dressing and swabs and beds for All The animals and citizens of the Kingdom of God, The All we each in turn have battered and robbed. And we shall then, finally, become like Christ: We'll begin washing feet and forgiving. And the healing shall be our healing.

Love (hence, life)

Love (hence, life)
How might I love You,
Love (hence, life) You?

A riotous mess, man,
Man wrinkled, a riotous
Wrinkled mess. Yet
You wouldn't iron it out
Smooth or finish (yet) it.
You bare it, wear it,
Love (hence, life) it.

How might I love (hence,
Life) it like You,
Love (hence, life) You?

16

    who would want to write
           poetries quite
                        legible?
i am greedy for words:
English is English and it is bursting:
i'll fix the canvas to the floor,
the wall, splash   drip   pour
                        paint over it all
avoid a point of emphasis;
besides, who writes
for those who lost
                a love of stories?
i'll fix the canvas to the floor.
        young virgins
                have much to say about sex—and the trees
        have lost their leaves but that makes
                    them all the more huggable!—if only
 because they haven't yet.
       i will write new poetries.
love and abstractions,
the sex I've never had—no more!
       i will write about two-by-fours,
the land, and civil war/ write between schism.
i will write with teeth.
i will lay iambic pentameter like joists and beams,
punctuation like galvanized nails,
verses like rafters hung high over hardwood floors.
        there I will bring you, laydee, there.
        on that floor i will,,,   ,   would you:

       a. kiss me up against the canvas
       b. call a cab
       c. fix a nicotine fit, and/or
            i. paint
            ii. rip-roaring
            iii. date kissing goodbye

clay eyes | Tyler Blanski

House painting

Forty feet up
On planks, cutting
Straight lines, fast lines, sure and trim.
We worked to finish the South Side
By noon, before the sun would bake
The paint to a cream
Five-gallon surface film,
Cake our brushes
And slow our lines all tacky.

We worked in twos, tag-teaming:
First all four, each two on trim, then separating
One for laps, leading,
And one to follow rolling, back-brushing:
Two on the left and two on the right,
Where we met, feathering.
The first to finish would roll tobacco,
Legs dangling forty feet up,
And smoke, bantering.

And then, all down:
Lower the ladders,
Adjust the jacks,
Empty another
Gallon into the Five and climb.
All four divide, dicing,
Climb two on either side,
Minds wandering the clapboard siding,
The satin finish blinding.

When did days learn boys' wants so?
To bend and heat their backs to a red umber,
Before each to his high and scut work would go?

Dearly

She pays, she pays dearly now.
Karats and cuts can't make a wedding band glitter.
Chewing the cud, too late, she contemplates how
Light caresses left her in the dark so embittered.
Her heavy breasts, her swollen stomach, her cramps:
He kisses her all over in a wonder and never asks,
Is it his? But is it his?

But yesterday they woke in the winter,
Made breakfast chattering like chickadees,
Cutting out the land they loved together.
Now she fears he'll hear the grinding of her teeth
Or the slow, lacerating heaves when she weeps
Behind the sound of the water in the shower,
But is it his? Is it his?

Those days could go on forever.
If she could but bear the weight upon her finger,
The weight that makes it hard to lift
Her hand to touch his cheek and kiss
The hair upon his head when he listens and drifts
Over her belly, ending to rest and think upon her chest.
Dearly now: not all, she thinks, is in forgiveness.

Life, select quotes

I once read, 'Life is one damned thing after another.' Others have as much muttered: 'When you wake up in the morning, smile and get it over with;' Or on God: 'A nasty surprise in a sandwich, a drawing pin caught in a sock.' And perhaps only because he was able, Yet another has buttered, 'Let us go then, you and I, When the evening is spread out against the sky Like a patient etherised upon a table.' And life seemed to me Godless and gloomy.

But then I read that life is like an old hag forever threatening to become beautiful; an old hag who 'put(s) a glass of cold cranberry juice, Like a big fake garnet, in your hand. Cranberry juice! You're lucky, on the whole, *But there is a great deal about it you don't understand.*' And elsewhere: 'I neglected to say my prayers but had good health, good thoughts, and good humor, thank God Almighty. I rogered my wife vigorously.' And again, 'Lord, thank you for the goddamn birds singing!' And life seemed to me full of pressing
     unbuttoned
         gladness
             gist
                 sing-song

clay eyes | Tyler Blanski

lemons

yr lips and hibiscus flowers, orange peel, and licorice root;
yr tongue and yr cinnamon, rose hips; yr lemongrass

and blackberry laugh (i like this very much)
to a lemon verbena, and then a

lemon balm
calm.

clay eyes | Tyler Blanski

if art would be love

    Since art is the opposite of hurry/
    is not like anything else in this world,

    if love would be art/
    be unlike everything else in this world,
    love will be slow, head scratching, scab picking.

    But if love would be art—
    art, full of exception and anomaly/ open
        to interpretation and perforation—then may it also Burst,
rush, bloom, Elope!

    And since art and science are complementing,
    may art learn science's daily proofs
    of God and demons and the tiers of Heaven
    and Hell and Earth/ may it start digging.

    And since art is science's equal, except never
    hurries to the moon; and science is less than love,
    which flutters above any cause-and-effect nexus,
    let art learn from love and start complimenting,
    which is the reverse side of everything else
    in this world/

clay eyes | Tyler Blanski

Transplanting

Grant, O Lord, the daily, hourly grace
To meet the daily, hourly.

I am planted in the dry spaces.
I suck water from the sand and
Fashion a god from a man.
But from here I can see a river. I would take root there.
Lord, give me a spade.

But not so fast: the blade is sharp!
I must consider my fragile roots.
I must not break them.
I wouldn't want scars. I—
Lord, get my mind off myself,
(even in the asking it, my mind bends on itself).
Lord, take away the spade.

And so He digs. He promised He would.
And all the while I pout and cry,
    I think I   see another way,
    I think I   found a gentler blade,
    I think I   need not be awake.
And my mind, a mess of mirrors, crowds working room.
Lord, where is the spade?

From here I can see a river. Lord, where is the spade?
I would take root there. Where is the spade?
Where did the gardener go?

Memento Mori

So, then: this…this what? Act of God?
She's gone. Neighbor children play on our lawn.
They don't ask for her: they don't understand
What: Fate? Nada? An uneven ending
For the sake of some divine drama? This,
This Chance? Time flipped tails and the universe can't give a damn?
Damn and double damn if four and four do not make two:

I can go days not knowing I live in the world,
Not hearing the music she plays—her lilt, her twirl.
We all go feet up. So, then: what?
Despite man's plans the earth is (and our lot) sapped still.
And I'm left to rummage through her (she's gone) old luggage, her
What she couldn't bring along.
I'll sit in a lawn chair at the garage sale and smile and nod.

Late I'll yawn back the salt in my eyes; and the nada,
The nada y nada. What? Milk and honey,
Growth and decay: men and women rise
From dirt to sing and die. A mist rose up from the garden.
One Arc in all the rain: a clean well lighted space;
Mulled wine and lamb; we try over jokes and times now gone;
And then I'll rinse dishes. A little quiet in the evening. So, then.

clay eyes | Tyler Blanski

when every critic is a cricket, and i can no more create

find me at your cabin

steeping wide-eyed

black coffee

by your sleepy fire of logs

we'll play cribbage till the moon lights the dell

where every cricket's song

is provéd penury

to the firefly's

dark erratic

      fifteen-two, fifteen-four

and a   double run   for twelve

clay eyes | Tyler Blanski

Uz

      —but I will not hold my tongue!
Am I some deep-sea snake-monster
that thou, thou grimsome watcher,
watch me even when I swallow my spittle?

Darkness is my couch; the worm, my mother.
I scrape my skin with scrap pottery. If I cry 'Murder!'
no one answers me; and when thou pass,
I cannot even see thee, thou crocodile!

As surely as the sparks whirl upwards
will that night which said, 'A man is conceived!'
keep breaking the silence of my open grave.
Thou hast made me thy butt. 'So be it.'

Supplicant

When childish,
I would walk through Red
Pine, Jack Pine, Aspen
To a quieting birch stand
And pray in threads,
Sway powerless.

Once
A carousing rain incensed
Swiftly crashed across
The lake and through the birch copse.
A dour Dionysus observance
Rushed

The branches,
Shook the leaves,
And set the birches swinging.
I remember, childish, listening.
I easily believed
The dances,

And heard
The birches laughing,
Clean, wet, shaking when it cleared:
When blue skies dried tittering tears.
I would stay, standing,
And turn

And turn,
Neck craned, looking up,
Up and up at all that swaying,
The moss and leaves staining
My shoes and pant cuffs.
Was all I asked unheard?

clay eyes | Tyler Blanski

27

Laydee, lie back. Rest your head
In my left hand, your breasts
(my laydee)

I would like to love you
The old-fashioned way
As one unfamiliar with the terrain
As one who in his unknowning
Is made all the more brave
(may I?)

I have known the pen days
The manila and postmen days
The you I could not touch, only read
Only lonelily write to in the winter *par avion*
I fell in love with your delicate, stabbing mind
With your anger and laughter and worry
How I would care, caring
Love, amass, lust; pray, all blurry

I wrote often. So many lettery words
My hands could do better, I'm sure
Find and lay you down
(my laydee, may I now?)

clay eyes | Tyler Blanski

A faerie for every boy and girl

Darling, when Children know so much
they don't believe in faeries—don't say it!
when look is not to see and listen is not to hear,
and when every man's a codfish!
why would you stay sleeping
in your bed when you could be
with me, saying silly things to the stars?
Then wear my kiss around your neck,
and I want your every thimble,
I'll keep your kiss inside my pocket to remember.

The first time a baby laughed
the laugh shattered into a thousand tiny pieces—
they're skipping all about us still: it's written
all over your very merry face!
when I carry you (that's what one does
                       with laydees, when the smallest
                       of all the stars in the Milky Way
                                   shouts 'Now!').
So we'll never never grow in look or hear too old,
I'll make—I will!—them stick on with soap:
a faerie for every boy and girl—don't say it!
and all the time for thimble smell and thimble taste;
for me to thimble you,
        for you and all your smiles, thimbling back.

What a funny treasure map, second to the right.
What a funny thing to say so gravely.

clay eyes | Tyler Blanski

a guggenheim dates an artist

he came to her apartment in the Spring of April 9
smelling of soap
tasting so potato
she should have had more condiments

he had a few roundabout words about her paintings
—ego, id, and superego, like every other wonder
bread piece of work in that city
she had a few high words about his cosmopolitan airs
—entirely poseur, like every other
two-martini-lunch arriviste in that city

she should have had more condiments
foaming non sequiturs
and looking so red-ripe tomato
he left her apartment circa the Summer of June 3

clay eyes | Tyler Blanski

Stratocaster stratosphere

Sometimes a man needs to rock out, he said,
and turned up Led Zeppelin. The sun setting

pushed through the thick trees and humidity,
filled the living room with July. Rock music in July.

He paced from the kitchen to the living room to the kitchen
to the deck, stared off in a happy By God! haze as if to say,

No matter What day is it? That night we stayed outside late
and drank cold canned beer in broken chairs long after

the record popped and crackled to a stop and scratched
and scratched and never asked Why, just scratched,

      under the loud and experimental anti-establishment sky.

Coupling

...then I was in his eyes as one who finds peace.
      —Song of Solomon

Your beauty, love, is not bound by the mundane mold.
But in every detail and in every fold
You surpass those static common souls
Who know not the meaning of art, love, or life to the full.

You and I, two poets at the pen
Laboring to articulate the sweetest lines of verse,
Striving to surmount the dissonance of the curse.
Together, lovers loving, and allowing nothing
To let this love reverse.

King David's Dance

And he'll tell you how to get there
By the rivers, not the highways.—Storyhill

I asked him once how to get there,
To his cabin in the mountains.
The smell of God and the open road—
Wind and mud tracked in,
Boots to stomp and roam…

Rumors roll down like folklore,
Salvation with no credit and paid in wrinkled tens,
Like an even' cloud rolling down into the foothills.
They clothe the fields in dew.

Smile undentisted smiles,
Tell unspoken tales:
There, still, campfires burn trees once pointed to the stars;
There, still, brews cowboy coffee and the old bard's song.
While their smoke rises, rumors roll down like mass,
Life with little syntax.
Bearded passion from every angle.
Something primeval.

I would show you a fist full of beans
But they leaped up into the welkin
    To dance with Orion
(Who still dances madly 'round our electricity).
There is no law of gravity.
    Only timothy hay.
Only word ringing through beauty bona fide.

clay eyes | Tyler Blanski

Late the candle burns

Late the candle burns,
Spilling wax and leaning like no one sees him:
The lumpy beautiful
Like old man's hands, like dirt under fingernails.
Labor to be one mind.
Love is like drawing hands.
Look: Listen: Lock it in your brain:
Knuckles and wrinkles and timelines,
Hands to draw hands;
Hands to touch and love the imperfection of the land.
Time, we have time.
Time dark and time full-bodied, time like gospel music.
Time for depth and sweetness and silliness…
Let our frolic be spontaneous and slow,
Top-shelf bourbon by the fire slow—
A taste to be lingered over, savored,
Subtle and smoky-flavored.
     Let it be like prayer—
    An idiom sown in garden rows,
    Soil-like, dirt-like. Till the land.
    Love is like drawing hands.
    But do not push and pry and grope.
    We are, each other, one young love ring
      Of simple sterling, not of gold.

clay eyes | Tyler Blanski

Clobbering father wings

My father is a child
who never stopped building forts,
never stopped playing in them.

He'd come home shouting
mother's praises/ praises to God,
praying for supper in incomplete sentences:
'Sky—Street—Casserole—Glory—Lord
—A-Beautiful-Wife-Who-Made-It—Amen!'

He is always sketching, sketching
doors and back roads and buildings;
sketching us, pretending not to care:
the subject in the foreground,
the prayer in the background:
he knows that to see is to pray
is to have wings.

Growing up we'd grumble at his curiosity
when he'd ask about our day, protest
when he'd never let us say none-of-it-matters.

He'd smack our backs
after supper when we'd wrestle.
We could hear the hard thuds
move through us, giggling;
percussive love taps as if to say,
'I-love-you! I-love-you! I-love-you!'

We're learning slowly how to hit back.

clay eyes | Tyler Blanski

I wanted to tell you

I wanted to tell you—to give you—but I—it's

written by—I mean, it's about you—me, that is—to say

what I mean is—you know, us—well, you and me—stop look

ing at me that way!—who said anything?—why did
you—I just wanted to tell you—

clay eyes | Tyler Blanski

i heard around a whispering

i heard around a whispering
fricative, plosive, devils' *f th k p t g b fthk*
our own ineed i see i hatei know

we do not know who surrounds us
whence our thoughts enter.

singing yesterday, 'come,
Lord Jesus;' i heard a refrain, softly
saints singing all around me
a thousand pastel strikes, like a flailing,
scribbling Degas/ children
holding crayons: 'come, Lord Jesus; come.'
i am weary on my own sing-a-long
the inky hand of David,
the sound of scribbling, the incessant
whispering.

clay eyes | Tyler Blanski

Individual, individual

forgive my violence, expansion,

pride. tides, sun reflections, gloss deep

pacific placid—beneath the green and warm,

down in the not-dead-but-dying, alive and molding.

i fill the vats/ pack the grain stores.

but when all has run its natural course—

after the piles and the lies and the impossible I

—a horse! a horse! my kingdom for a horse!

Senior citizens

When senior citizens start splash ing in pudd les,

and hoary old women let down their gray hair;

when every old man brandishes his sword and cudgel

and takes to bellow ing as he plays or sits in his chair;

when every dodder ing one of them gives up on fashion,

and all the busy young and sexy bow as they proudly pass,

will mort ally man kind re claim her dignity , her nobility.

clay eyes | Tyler Blanski

Cedar

I never break a branch when I walk the woods.
Though one afternoon I cut a cedar bow for whisking

in the sauna, to shock and scratch the surface of the skin
in the sauna. Foolishly, I left the branch inside to wither all evening

as I stoked the fire from the outside, coaxing the tight cabin
to a high eucalyptus 190°. That evening I whisked my cousin

with the skeletal binding, and strewed its dried pages everywhere.
My morning chores then included the cleaning of the sauna.

It took me hours to gather the torn scraps left carpeting the floor.

I never break a branch when I walk the woods;
Though I might pinch a folio from a bow to roll in my hands,

cup my hands, and lift to smell and to read the stories it tells.
The Ojibwe say the Cedar is sacred: and I believe them—that was a yarn

woven the old way, before the pail and the axe and the lumber yards
threw wheat up, forgetting to sift the grain from the chaff, scattering

stories everywhere. They will never tell again. But walking,
the woods (though not forgetting) forgive, and still play at storytelling.

clay eyes | Tyler Blanski

My brother's hands

My brother's hands are a big
gentle thing, a restless confident thing,
like his mind.
                    When he talks,
always so practically profoundly plain,
you secretly (always) agree—

though you'd never admit it, just to watch him squirm
and vex and say in such a tender obvious way,
'No.'
                    My brother's hands
are a wondered dexterous thing, like his heart,
a delicate strong and moving thing,

a thing to shape a paper plane (and all things) well,
to open the globe, and set it all soaring

out and up to the hands of the Maker.

clay eyes | Tyler Blanski

None righteous; no, none.

      —Let us
hold God true, even if every man be proved
a liar!—
        Man is but the plaything of his desires—
Men's secret lives—we are spiders
    over the fire
        —better one righteous man's silence
            than a hundred loveliest of these
                    —Beauty is rarely Truth,
and the Scavenger of Heaven elbows through the crowds and cans
      —prods, pulls out
every blonde with a butterfly tattooed on her back,
      every bottle or cigarette with a Joe affixed to it; any who creep
out under black clouds and roundabouts,
  Winter rains, a picture of Gabriel the archangel,
    And Christ the Pantocrator,
Fingers raised to bless teach reach—any who wonder awe
shake their heads—
    Plead laud God make me pliable!
—I am no more or less the rest the blest
    the mess the curse's worstest.

clay eyes | Tyler Blanski

Be thou now my only

But when Spring is Winter and Morning is Midnight,
Will you call? Will you write your Stars to come courting?

And when Six is Seven and Twelve is Eleven,
Will you sleep well? Will you nap in the Afternoon Light?

O, do not
Say, Nothing!

When I'm a muddling fair to middling Mess and all Horse Apples,
Do not hesitate. Do not tell the Sea Shells to stop shoring.

Rather, be thou now my only every Green Thing,
My Well and my Moon/ Rain Drops and Dew only;
Shell cluttered shores: drop on my tongue
Every honey dripping Thought—

O God, you are my God, you are   my   God,
And I am yours, I am yours, I   am   yours.

clay eyes | Tyler Blanski

Rocks to moan and clench

Eli, eli, lema sabachthani. And then an empty quiet,
Like the quiet before an Atom Bomb
                                        dropped. A shudder.
The earth rolled over, a patient on her sick bed
Groaning, clenching her teeth, afraid her stomach might heave—
And the curtain forked in quiet,
Like the quiet of a half-empty wedding bed.
                                        No warmth on his side,
The made-in-words in Wordlessness.
A moan beneath a char-green sky.
Eli, eli, lema sabachthani

For three days the womb did not recognize herself.
Hourglass whores and toothless whispers.
Under blankets she thrust the knife, bloodied the pillows,
Looked down, saw she was still naked from kisses
                                        and ran madly into the sty.
The rocks have moaned and do not forget why.
Eli, eli, lema sabachthani.

Why still the laughing time under blankets and sheets?
Why still the thousand kicking babies in wombs?
Why still the breast, the rocking chair, or the table?
And why still the fields heavy and white?

Because he woke. Because he touched the concave of her tired waist,
Smoothed back her hair and poured kisses on and on her face.
Because the blood soaked through the floorboards,
                                        flooded the fundament.
Because we hear the squeal of a hundred pigs in the distance,
And though gasping, now have breath to sing.

Kiss the earth, then, the earth He sowed in garden rows.
Break the black-blue earth for planting. Throw out the rocks
(That we should give them reason to clench and moan again!)
Plant little seeds for little people.
And sing with new, bagpipe-like lungs.
Eli, eli, lema sabachthani rings our springtime, our Eastertide, life begun.

clay eyes | Tyler Blanski

clay eyes | Tyler Blanski

clay eyes | Tyler Blanski

clay eyes | Tyler Blanski

clay eyes | Tyler Blanski

www.ingramcontent.com/pod-product-compliance
Lightning Source LLC
Chambersburg PA
CBHW031656040426
42453CB00006B/324